SOME
SEMBLANCE
OF
DECAY

BY

BRENDAN TRIPP

THE CAGE WHICH GRASPS AND CHAINS

so beaten down
lost in destruction's path
all deeds are pointless
they are swept away
by tides of madness,
neutralized
by compensating waves
which leave all blank

this is the web of change
in which rules loss
everything we've had now fades
into an absence
a dripping void
an emptiness torn from the form
of what was once before
and can never be again

we, dutiful, enact the patterns
which seem to have been new ordained
but in a darkness,
not like the path,
a cloaking mist which would confuse
and leave us wandering on planes
which are uncharted
and have no end

the strictures of this time
rise up and madden
we are neither here nor there
neither up nor down
somehow in states still undefined
which find us clawing for the door
into a structured zone
where we could learn the lines

new phases paralyze
we lose direction
and can not shake the chain
reappearing on our hands
this grows a prison out of air
a dungeon from a meadow
a cruel confinement
from what had been release

WHEN JOURNEYS ARE ALLOWED TO GO

so many things destroyed
such precious things retained
we drift against the current
run by mysteries
we encompass ancient knowings
and are given leave to change
these into something new

it is not the standard way
we are all outlaws on this road
bundled against doctrines
which seek to freeze and slay
leaving all as sculpture
and idolaters' delight

metal bands are breaking
chains pull out from stone
there is a chaos in the breath
which would blow houses down
scattering the face cards
into courtyards of the blade
leaving without leaders
a void which needs be saved

all these things we've captured
how soon might we digest?
too many plans are swirling
to predict a single one
too many lines are weaving
to be able to trace roots
in the tangle of the sight

movement shifts the focus
to what bears stasis still
we track behind the veils
what does not surface stir
but generates these eddies
in the tide beneath the time

every visage
every face
offers us a portal
to reach inside the mind
and taste the knowing
the book of days
these chronicles of being
for purposes unsaid

THIS PIN HOLE IN THE HIDE

1
so much clutter
so many voices
many scenes
there is no focus
we can not center
we can't achieve the state
which is the aspect
defining need
2
blocked and stymied
all roads are walled
all pathways sealed
each attempt is useless
each exertion failed
to break out of this void
and enter other systems
we're sure reside outside
3
fallen from belief
we run in circles
hamster in our cage
taken to the wheel
so much is spent here
for so little gain
a forward vector leading
across a too-curved space
4
we find the names
of what is not
and see the surface
of what will be
but can not jostle
the potential into real
can not turn
the corner into light
5
this calm is shattered
we grind more than before
the hours dwindle
that can be optioned free
and we are twisting
down tunnels of recall
which lead to nowheres
yet ones where we have been

TRACKS OF THE DRIFT

these elements decay
we are set apart
unable to attain

the other side
is taken away
we can not reach

something new
is so afar
gone to indistinction

these aspects turn
within this frame
all open

contrasting zones
return to steel
without resistance

it is empty
it is old
beyond the count

the words escape
they are so few
that reside

sacred ground
does not contain
the good recall

we fade
drift back
subside

subsistence is
a split in time
gone crazy

IN LATENESS RAGE

too many things of need
we always tell
the hours build too high
where waits our sleep?
this is damning,
this is dark
we can do nothing
yet have so much to do

under anguish
resides a hate
we loathe these chains
that keep appearing
like stigmata on our wrists
we tear them off
but they surface there again
mocking our dreams of flight

killing days
twisted times
we turn so lethal
poisoned dead inside
and wait to spread the bane
on an all-deserving world
which shall taste putrescent rage
so long awaiting shape

are tomorrows more like these?
we reject them then
we tear away
all the stupid things of man
and cast all to the pit
I will not be under this yoke
I will not live this insane game
there will be death before

so deep the loathing
of that sick race
so hard resentment
of those so blind
I wait revenge upon their deeds
to sweetly savor
the opening of eyes
too much inured to sleep

THESE LOCALES FRAMES

reach across
grasp air
nothing here
nothing real

these are absences
they're what we feel
they're the gaps
between being and percept

so many cycles
with no control
so many vectors
without a map

an alteration fades
a placement shifts
a spiral enters
without exit

will completion come?
what dawn brings stasis
to these shores
so long in sudden flux?

what doing makes
not finding done
what intent builds
from stuff of dreams

almost sleeping
so like the rest
confounded now
with all the blind

a structure hovers
out of sight
behind strong veils
waiting to uncloak

clear vision
is given us again
we see beneath
and plumb the depths of man

in fleeting
and moments' fill
turned empty
without the key

GONE THROUGH THESE CHANNELS

1
the silence swells
and takes position
high upon the hills
we are surrounded
locked amid the calm
no order utters
no command conducts
in this gathered zone
2
we swim to shores
which are unnamed
and trace the context
in which these natives bide
we scrawl a message
upon those sands
to open pathways
across that sea
3
floating in between
there is no grounding
we drift on currents
shafts of air
approaching doorways
which have no key
traversing hallways
which have no end
4
again the waking dream
the sharp return
as though we dreamt this way before
and should be able to skip ahead
cut to the chase
pass by the cup
and reappear
resplendent in the final phase
5
so now we ask
what we ourselves can't do
place down demands
in the neutral turf before
and see what weapons
are brought to bear
in hard respondings
and harsher need

WHEN IS NOT THE DREAM?

it enables nothing
there is little there
we transgress
the bounds of new constraint
and take back darkness
as a comfort and a cloak
wrapping the nighttimes
as solace round the soul

something enters
something comes to call
we see its visage
in the imprint on the screen
hear its murmurs
beneath unsubtle winds
and sense its moving
in the shadowplay of light

we gather systems
maintaining edge
there are contradictions
between expectations
and the real
we walk into the hardness
and grasp unyielding stone
knowing that its truth shall last

set apart from instance
we are woven through recall
a mat of past occurrence
which floats about in time
we are shuddered by the absence
of what is held as sure
unable yet to fathom
how these things all go lost

we wait that waking
when things are clear
when every action
confirms to driving will
and not to vagueness
the hollowness of now
so deep in failing
so locked into false states

GONE TO THE GRINDER

there it goes,
the crashing,
the downfall,
we knew it was near
from the creaking
and groaning in the walls
the rumbles in the ground
and the shadows on the plane

so many lies...
we fail in will
can not achieve
our weak intents
we wallow
in a mire too deep to stand
caught by its suction
pulled to our deaths

here are the millions
that scream for doing
here are myriads
which now insist
we have to pare away
what little flesh we can
but find each cut
has newly slain

the mind is pressured
and seeks escaping
every turn
brings new concern
new twisting deadlines
new warping drives
fresh forms of terror
to strain the eye

a vision beckons
a state awaits
a place beyond
a zone within
another time
where these can't go
a different day
than of our capture

CURSED THINGS UNMADE

1
what is not attained
what is not achieved
what is not absorbed
what is not absolved
such stare
from mirrors reflect
gaze from glass
accuse from steel
2
we can not see beneath
the surface of this plane
we can not adjust
dimensions to our mind
to grasp the greater frame
and see the wider span
we can not know the ways
abiding in the world
3
the drift
is not the journey
the sinking
is not found depth
the show
is not in learning
the vision
is not revealed
4
we reach nothing
in hazy times
all structures blend
into unfinished webs
layer upon layer
translucence into grey
and certain being
into doubt and fear
5
every act has fallen
every system dies
every door is sealed against us
every option fades away
there's no snapping
out of this
there's no rising
from this line

THE CEASELESS GRIND

hollow voices
empty sight
we drag against the sand
and are hampered
we run across the tide
and expire

storms abate
clouds drift away
their baggage packaged
and then stored
their systems lifted
and forgotten

too many plans
within thin time
there are no promises
which can be kept
there are no reasons
which abide

drifting down
sinking to the depths
our passage is destructive
it crushes us with mass
our voyage goes on endless
denying us a rest

each vector pure
each arrow poisoned
no pointers offer up a guide
only lines' interpretation
no patterns structure webs
and yet they capture

held by bias
steel in the flame
only pressure issues light
within this burial
only pressure turns the wheel
which opens eyes

GONE TOWARDS DOWNWARD SPINS

from darker states
we arise
we delve into this lore
and break the code
we shuffle through the lies
to find the hidden truth
we split apart the time
to our dismay

the storm has gathered
and shudders every pane
we have nothing here
we are emptied
poured out on planes
so parched, so arid
welcoming the blood
no longer ours

echoes of the legend
flash from hidden sites
so unexpected
and twisted round
they bring to mind the carcass
which waits in realms of heat
to bring us back again
if only by its stench

now we walk the path
which has no guidance
we seem the fool
but are only in the rut
there are no exits
which lead to safe aways
this is no journey
but a death march we must take

pain in many vectors
blindness all around
no focus have we
no point to fix
there is a madness in the tide
a chaos in the form
which has no mercy
and drags us down again

IN OTHER SIGHTS

now we make new strides
into the darkness
now we leap
from parapet heights

what nightmare surrounds us
and keeps hooks in our mind?

it is evil
we feel it
we know it
it is a horror
based on some other time
which has followed
our footsteps to this place
thinking we'd forgot

so far we've gone
yet not released
the prayers still rise
for loosing chain

the maelstrom pulls
it cycles down
dragging all
into its sway
we are desperate to swim
to calmer shores

this is not the way it's meant to be
this is not the pattern of all dreams

what is linked within
shall not go asunder
we shall delve into the eyes
which see the past as now
and look out into light
which has really yet to shine

so many things derail here
hurtle off into the sand
to rust and fade
dwindle and decay

now turn the handle
expecting more the wheel

SHARP SOUND TAKEN

1
geysers of history
flooding mental planes
tearing at remembrance
sweeping out our context
2
weakness grips
shallow forms infect
and shift around the line
which points to will
3
so unstuck in time
there is no focus
no center to compare
or anchor all these days
4
thousand foot walls
sheer black granite
a million miles too wide,
how is passage made?
5
images cede images
illusions twist the mind
and we find layered chain
no longer in the sights
6
forgotten phrases
notes which won't recall
every vast expanse
the scent of things once seen
7
an emptiness pervades
an ache crawls through
leaving trails of anguish
and sorrow as its slime
8
what changes
when nothing is the same?
what enters
in absoluted void?

THE CALL

two millennia of madness
the ages of the Lie
born of a winning heresy
that has trampled down the truth
two thousand years of murder
leaves blood stains on their hands
that can't be washed by water
only by this night

time to turn the cycle
time to wield the blade
time to tear the facade down
and commit it to the flames
the hour now is ready
the balance is on edge
Earth only waits the man of will
to issue the command

we see the cyclone building
the shift in deeper tides
the returning of the answers
on the storm front of the mind
now is the point of lightning
that opens up closed eyes
now is the spark of terror
that illuminates the real

damned are those believing
what's been passed down as true
damned are those dependent
on comfort without light
damned are those who follow
the Liar's twisted words
damned are those defending
a too-corrupted Church

it is the night of chaos
before the knowing dawns
a time of blood and carnage
to be savored by the strong
that morrow brings a new day
and a new race that would see
what has been long occluded
but now returns to free

DOWN FROM WAITING

1
there be monsters here
there be nightmares waiting
we can't scan enough
to even see
we can't extend reach
to foment grasp
there is a darkness down
there is a shift to falling
2
broken out of return
set liminal
not ungone
not arrived
divided from intention
dropped into modes
which have no labels
no way to know or act
3
rejecting systems
we haunt vast tombs
placed as though a specter
unable to connect
we drift through phases' calling
not reaching for the light
which hides beyond forever
a rumor in these darks
4
strange channels pull us
echoing the past
making us believe
what won't exist
swelling up with visions
of what has never been
layering the mystery
of emptiness maintained
5
no remember
all forgot
no achieving
all descent
no existence
all to void
no decision
all reroute

AWAITING LATER SPADES

these assignments
move so slow
there is mist which clings around us
and memories that impair
with vague confusion
and tracks we wish to trace
into tomorrows
which we should never see

histories resurface
and gasp as if for air
we wait a changing
when masks will fall away
leaving open
every surprise
framing distance
as the central need or care

in darkness settled
without the script
we hazard strange surrounds
and systems we don't know
in interest of a future
which is structured if not planned
unfolding in a zone state
where every space is filled

there are gaps within
our lines have lies
which lead to visions
of what has never been
we grow polluted
with many pretty songs
but know the dirge is coming
within the somber tide

the wave now hovers
high up in the sky
its roar has silenced
all in expectation
soon comes the crashing
that sweeps away
soon comes the chaos
which is the theme of days

UNDER KILLING BLADES

1
anguish grinds
hours drag
scenarios bloom
in line with dread
2
burned and sere
so alone
we wait the sun
to bleach our bones
3
outside cycles
locked to loss
stripped of motive
in panic's way
4
on and on
down and down
is there no ending,
no final say?
5
calendars demand
schedules insist
we shift the context
as though to whim
6
the separation
is tinged with fear
what might remain
upon return
7
the mind arrays
with strange recall
image against image
form against strange shape
8
now a passage
opens up
a path in darkness
and chill like ice

OF DICTATES AND DURATION

1
these run with it
they take velocity
and hurtle down the mountain
cascading down the hills
and rushing through the valley

2
what can not be made
we know no system
we have no aspect
from which to build
it is a nightmare here within
where all is hollow
acid-eaten and decayed

3
nobody accepts this
no one will see the true

4
it is of the time
run cycles
bleeding memory
harried in return
we have nothing there
but these delusions
stacked in anger
and left to dry

5
all the answers freeze
and become new doctrine
all the questions fade
and become denied

6
what can be saved?
what can be known?
do passing points of light
lose all holdings?
do fractions of the night
span the real?
even then:
it is not enough to be within this
it is not enough to have this goal

BOXES PAST THE FILLING

1
such progresses low
such descends beneath

2
feinting into vistas
which were not there before
opening into mythos
which cannot be attained

3
the structure aligns
the form is evolved
into stranger shape
flowers blooming metal
blue to steel and guns
lethal with intent

4
they forget now
why they came
they lose lines
which can lead them back
tracking through the hallways
down the curves
past the dungeons
of these nights

5
elements derive
of distillates of blood
mixed with glowing stone;
what is retained
can not be sold
or bartered in the sun

6
another pause unkempt
within dictation
who becomes the wave
when all is swept?

7
now to shades appearing
what was it we said?

FRAMED WITHIN THE STAGE

1
it is unbelieved
and empty
these shells
blow across the plain
seeking root
seeking peace
but on terms
unable to be found
2
the swift
still are blind
the blind
still hold reins
of power in this world
there is a fire
they can not see
a flame which shall burn
3
other facets
have turned into the light
they glisten, newborn
we watch the mirrors
to know these lines
which grow hardened
exposed to befouled air
miasmas of the lie
4
this bleeding has no end
we float on seas
tapped from our veins
red awash
thick, too warm, and vile
magnets stir a current
which is not ours
leading us aground
5
the fever grabs
the madness grows
talons develop
there on the other side
waiting for the tearing
the rending of the veil
the moment of pure violence
when everything descends

SO CAUGHT WITHIN THE TRAP

these horrors enfold
they wrap reality around us
stifling the breath
twisting off the light
driving panic to the soul
until nothing seems
and nothing works
and nothing is attained

these monsters
none can see them
yet they thrust talons through the heart
and eviscerate the gut
they shred the skin
and pound the brain to gel
in incessant beating
the unrelieved attack

we walk through gauntlets
made of blades
pass down hallways
strung with cutting wire
ride the crest
of acid waves
dissolving in the backwash
melting in the slag

Hell holds no promise
worse than the realm of Man
no demons lurk beyond
viler than those here
no tortures wait in death
which seed more pain than these
we are damned into this world
and cursed that we might see

the hours pass
and new nightmares come to rise
unsuspected battles
which have no way to win
pursuits through the mind
of ever-damning frames
which grasp us in their context
and grind us till we bleed

DOWN AND EVER DOWN

so many fallings
so deep the drop

no bottom here
things expand
through very tiny points
we lose everything
and yet don't shift
we expire
and yet arise

too much whirling
too many returns
we ache to define
what has no edge

what grasp can hold,
what thought can frame?
there is too much to being
to know it from within
only blindness leads us
to say what something is

set apart
the tides still pull
involuted
still explosion drags

something is unspoken
some pattern still maintains

missing dates
missing points
missing visions ripped from time
hoping that these levels
are stronger than the dreams
hoping that those actions
track on the greater screen

everything becomes
yet is touched by hands of death
sabotaged unfolding
flawed in every sense
infected and unclean

THIS DEPRIVATION RAG

disassociated
in free fall
floating
across this grid
no coordinates
no X no Y
no 2 nor time
to tag a zone

we can't attain
there is no reach
the journey goes
without the path
we see the echoes
writ out in pain
the anguish spray
upon the mind

something else becomes
it is not we
an evolution takes
what was not formed before
these tendrils point
and seek for liquids
following them we know
what feeds the vast facade

concrete images
shift across the field
welling and spinning
unfolding and slow fade
colors are a shape
sounds bear texture
deep within
the accessed soul

not released
nor resolved
something unravels here
and leaves this chaos
too many planes to sort
facets upon facets
twists confounding line
never with an end

NOTHING HERE TO HAVE

the mountain is moved
the sea is drained
the sky is swept
the planets stored away
how come
there is no completion?
how come
there is no sense of worth?

it is a trap
without a clue
it is a maze
that has no map
whatever we do
we somehow fail
no matter the height
it's not enough

blackness hovers
darkness touches
cold icy fingers
reach through the chest
they warn of a leaving
that none of these know
they speak of a jolting
from out of this world

it is nighttime
in the nightmare
it is shadowed
in ill dreams
too many trends
move in these lines
and everything points downward
into despair and decay

all our good
now rots
all our prayers
are mocked
all our plans
fall down
all our visions
false hope

PLUMMETED ABYSS

it becomes impossible
too much is gone
worlds slip away
trails of sand
through fingers gnarled
and twisted up in pain

no good remains
no hope survives
we are slaughtered
and crushed beneath these wheels
fodder for their mocking
tortured by these dreams

this is an emptiness
which leaves a scar
this is a void
which stinks of blood
this is a darkness
not of the womb

everything erases
all things cherished
are destroyed
mind can not hold
what is beloved in the world
and so falls to despair

the vectors move
as by some plan
armies on a map
yarn within the loom
knotting of the noose
on the gallows of this life

no waking comes
no brighter dawn
to strip away the lies
and open up the doors
this destruction
so soon shall be complete

BOTHERED FOR DESCENT

so many things
suck the force
bleed the will
so many things
steal the soul
tear asunder
self from intent
being from aim

this is corruption
this is decline
the world ensures it
the race is hardwired
for this decay
going foul in sunshine
turning vile by night
and all points in between

some semblance of resistance
creeps through the mind
a perversion
a contempt
hating what the outside is
despising all the others
whose existence forms a pull
a gravity on down

we can not touch the distance
which is solely what we need
we can not gain the substance
which is promised to our fate
we can not have the essence
which opens up the light
we can not grasp the presence
which is lurking behind veils

something is awry
turning from the frame
we pass on vectors
that should have met
we shift through lines
that once were one
we draw apart
without the why

THE POINT WHERE FRICTION IS

such tides
of resentment
of disdain
of flight
and aching
for further flight to be
more distant
stranger
greater
wider

these things we plan
are a facade
we dance around abysses
and stare into their depths
seeing others' eyes
so alien
so foreign
so contrary to what we are
in that hidden space
where shelters truth

we would let this shatter
fall to debris
but for our words
vows clear made
if only in one side
and not mirrored here
in dusty windows
which will be run from
and not cleaned
so like the mind

it is a darkness
it is a cage
it is a nightmare
whose tortures are unknown
each page now turning
to new unpleasantries
the metal chafes at us
the manacle of worlds
which will not leave us be
but always seek to slay

APART WITHIN APART

added disruption
we scan the skies
seeking seams
ways of tearing
the notch for fingers
to see what lies behind
the stars and depth
and empty black

we hone the blade
and search the target
one strike must kill
before the monster rises
all flame and fire
madness, blindness,
and centuries of lies
to strike us down in turn

before the journey
set on the trek
how does one breathe?
what can compare
with places distant
close to suns
rarified
so high

it is all forgotten
we weave these lines
but know no names
we walk the path
but lose the map
fatalness is
the locking of step
the fixing of eye

so many deeds
fly around this place
their shells,
skins, and skeletons,
in every dance
proclaim no leaving
only gravity
and the deepest things yet held

PERFECTING THE DECEIT

nothing works
function fails
drifting downward
into cold
into fall
into winter's grasp
and all the sounds
which ice the soul

we do not know
what voice there is
we have forgotten
all the gods
there is no trace
within us
touched so hard
and still unmarked

a dream behind the veil
a hope beneath the true
so many things reside
in these darkened corners
so many beings lurk
deep in the heart
this one tears us
brings tears unbidden

little wheels turn
at the edges
machines we can not see
works we can not know
which wax and fade
slipping from dimension
dropping out of time
once the need's complete

two hands waiting
for what must be revealed
the vision sharpens
honed on hardest stone
the will is steeled
for chaos and destruction
berserker in a world
which doesn't know its kind

THESE WE KNOW

such blood
such exit
these have blades
lines too fine
they sever
impale
subdivide
make history

which parts
have we purchased?
the fire takes all
sweeps up
consumes
others do this
we are distance
separate

structure moves
cement weaves
look beneath
see the web
unsuspected
unperceived
we trace this
make it ours

too much light
too many lies
counter currents
swell within the sea
creating vacuums
regions less dense
or too deeply dense
to not be solid

we descend to teach
and loathe the act
we appear to change
and recoil from touch
the pattern is too broken
the mirror is shattered
the function runs disjoint
within its closing

THIS ALIEN ANGST

these things destroy
they break ragged
smash chunks
from high facades
scattering shrapnel
across the plain
in the grey
in the agony

none know this
none see
we stumble among the blind
careen past their stares
searching a way to free
to flee
these bonds
this world

all systems falter
all rules collapse
there is no light
there is no grasping
we bleed more than dry
we are drained
of life, of hope
of even dreams

too many things
impinge the day
too many trails
beg follow
we can not trace
the paths behind
the vapor leaving
the arrow crossing time

such anguish
such pain
this is central
this is mine
isolated
no others feel
no others know
no others see

SOME OTHER PLACING

broken times
these split off
shatter on hard ground
nothing is known
little is sensed
we fail and scatter
dragging marks in sand
never to be tracked

shadowed patterns
are overlaid on acts
systems of recalling
echo other lines
making doubt encloud
as though the dream must be
realer than the day
and the waking state

too many murmurs
shudder round within
a chorus of supposition
of history and mind
which weave no webbing
expose no truths
give us no guidance
yet still seem to mean

how much goes forgotten?
we can not link the points
but can speak of stasis
lost between roads
we can not recite the life
which is given
but spew the words
intrinsic to the dark

when they shuttle
over these dry bones
kicking up the dust
will they know the vision
or only the dance?
will they sense the distance
which tears the soul
or only pain apart?

THIS STRUCTURE OF DECAY

the things of value
are lost
the cut of swords
too deep
we bleed
days curdle and crust
gore and putrescence
the darkest of vile

we hear sweet echoes
and know none others
can sense this
we touch near dreams
but they fade
upon horizons
point of impinging
point of attain

not enough is held
we walk in vapor
space goes grey
not even void
memory collapses
spilling out the past
through shattered walls
splintered glass

no good is
no blessings form
hallucinations linger
drive roots through souls
and ache for our belief
that we would stumble
in some blindness
so like the rest

here comes the chaos
here comes the reign
the steel ones are approaching
the dark ones are at hand
their madness infects
spreading through that sleep
till none are pure
none clean of that stain

GONE DOWN TO GRAYER STATES

such transmission goes
the pattern change
descent, decay
too known
our prayers
too empty
hollow ringing
bouncing from walls
the glassy dome
on which projections are

fears bob on the waves
they are the flotsam
upon the matrix of stress
they are the bloody chunks
flowing from the mulcher
they are the putrescence
flowing from eyes
black and horrid
rampant and insane
pressing inward at each hand

ribbons flow from sticks
vectors fluttering
unable to trace
unable to be defined
who can speak the symbol
really made herein?
too many simplifications
too much shorthand
too many want believing
to be supplanting truth

our acts all fail
we mock ourselves
to beat the crowd
to drown out their roar
with our own snide derision
blade for blade
blow for blow
we slay ourselves
to give satisfaction
to the bloodlust of the world

ON CUSPS OF DIREST FATE

desperate times
the season of anguish
we are glacial
and can not move

too many things
glisten on peripheries
we watch their play
and are so lost

desire has patterns
but just in mist
nothing gels here,
forms a whole

our absence staggers
we bleed the sea
cut by wounds
that never heal

flesh rots off
knowledge falters
all those pasts
have gone to dust

we reach down
and find no base
there is no substance
on which to build

other roads forgotten
sing dirges in the mind
like the siren
they lure our step

we can't learn how to be
we have no context
we are adrift
in ether more like foam

the swinging balance
now comes the time
for shaping something
or none at all

WHAT EXISTS AS PLAN

thus ensues the chaos
we shall be revenged
there is horror within
and terror without
there are nightmares
which shall not be contained
there are madnesses
which come to spread

we forget everything
we lose all also
only the rage maintains
only the killing drive
makes each day motive
to tear them down
to twist their world
to eradicate the norm

the gears turn
the numbers spill
how many deaths
are needed
how many places
do decimals shift
in the decimation
in the deluge?

blackness hovers
a night unseen
their own acts
craft the dark
their own lies
hone the blade
their own faith
feeds the fires

the only light
hides within
encased in crystal
it waits the bloom
shredding through the veil
burning through the sleep
ripping into eyes
unwilling to have seen

LOST WITHIN OUR SPACE

drastic meaning
twisted sense
we can not align
the disparate edges
can not assemble
the fractured chunks
into a semblance
into a whole

altered pattern
without key
no understanding gels
no structure surfaced
in the subsidence
this ebb
gone again in cycles
still so strange

touch what's been forgotten
see what's been denied
it is a distance
which has unraveled
it is a substance
which has arrived
treasured and precarious
warped in any shape

drifting outbound now
with no control
we see all prayers perverted
and all intents destroyed
we grasp at floating straw
but nothing here exists
which will support us
will save us from this grave

an absence follows
a darkness waits
the universe drops off
like the trap beneath the noose
we plummet dreading
the sudden violent snap
which brings the horror
all black and full of bile

A BOOK UNWRITTEN

from that vision
from that sense
we are tested
grilled afar
made to answer
for states unknown
set out plainly
in the day

words flow
and become truth
they pattern
they align
we wait the acting
which forms the frame
but this is distant
and not at hand

how might this
be basis made?
too many threads
run through the mind
to filter out
the main from side
the momentous
from the momentary

it is without need
yet is desired
it is without rule
yet is determined
we know its substance
on all too many lines
but can't find histories
to usher it in

when this comes
a new age rises
born of webs
woven out of light
cast across a sleeping race
pull tight, bejeweled
brighter than these suns
echoed in all myth

NOT EVEN OLD T.V.

misdirected reason
we burn in sun
we see these heights
we know of ways
too distant to be ours
but yet they're calling
us to that place
suspended out of time

elements' contrivance
form these shapes
we misinterpret
into frames
wire projections
symbols in the mind
which hold a trace
of reality inside

distinction offers
and sets a lure
we must filter
against those ways
walk in pureness
impeccably
not as center
but as core

every saying shapes
like chisels on the stone
every word
leaves impressions
which will not fade
the course is set
the die is cast
and time spills out aligned

some other aspect
is in the stream
it moves the flow
and channels light
we only drift
along that course
not steering, aimed
or sure to guide

ALL THAT GOES UNSEEN

so few options
so much denial
these cycles weave
a tapestry of death
a web of confusion
which catches us
and leaves us blind
and stagnant

bitterness runs
like glaciers melting
from frozen hate
and twisted rain
into the pools of despair
and hopelessness
that seek to drown
leaving no trace of us behind

no achieving
no clear line
we shift between
the unmarked hall
and the dungeon cell
between the exile void
and the world of chain
with no means of escape

snapshot freeze
mid-fall
mid-plummet
we seek some clue
to the depths below us
we seek some plan
which would arrest
the screaming downward tear

it is nightfall for this plane
tides are shifting beneath space
which stir the stuff of time
and leave us eddied patterns
which to the sensing eye can tell
what moves into our lives
these omens are uncheery
bespeaking deeper darks

WEBS OF DISSONANCE

this confusion
this chaos

there are no lines
no connecting dots
there are no forms
no way to function

it is descending
it is decay
it has an emptiness
which burns like acid
and twists the fibers
waiting for a snap

these systems falter
we stare at void
they have no future
all is hazardous
each door hides chasms
vertiginous drops
deep to the abyss
so hard and hateful

everything turns grey
swimming into black
the stars fade
the streets blur
nothing has purpose
nothing has aim

down amid the mass
we sense their sleep
we feel its weight
and can not bear

darkness infiltrates
we lose all light

NOT THE COURSE ONCE DREAMED

disturbing shifts
we bleed out color
exude corrupted form
warp with every factor
and descend within decay
    there is nothing left
    none echo
    from those pasts

we almost forget
what was the essence
we nearly lose
the structure of vision
    joining others
    deeply in their sleep
it is set apart here
distant but not far

so many changes
follow patterns
which go untraced
lacking gauges
needing lines
by which to true
these phantom shapes
not evolving

voices won't allow
hope to surface
our prayers are faces
pale beneath the wave
    cycles tighter
    run faster, spin
    seeding madness
    chaos, panic, rage

it is the chamber
opening from the hall
the sudden expanse
which stuns the gut
not allowing stasis
dropping into void
    vertiginous
    unquoted

DAMNED FUNCTION OF THE NIGHT

these bleedings
take down the soul
we are drained
of every purpose
emptied of all will
cut off from vision
and from the voice of light
once strong within

storms forever
rage on this place
no one sees
the grey and tearing sky
no one feels
the icy ripping wind
they do not know
the terror of these days

space forms a vortex
lines twist
spin and pull
dragging down
towards some nadir
a singularity of despair
which gapes as the abyss
eager to consume

we are broken
from the mesh
we are shattered
out of matrixes
of the native state
set apart in limbo
bordered by this void
unable to retrieve

strange gravities
set hooks into the gut
and shred away at form
warping essence
into a tortured mask
distorting spirit
into a mocking shade
which passes as the real

DROPPING CROSS MEMBRANES

beaten structures
insane minds
the stasis
is broken
the plane
sheets off
forming cliffs in desert
emptiness abrupt

some ancientness
calls us
some hallowed zone
is lure
but we are lost here
and have no map
we stumble through the denseness
thick with blinding fogs

our efforts build
in essence
they have no focus
no point in solid states
all these hours
drive virtual frames
beyond the basis
and into light

so much is bled
we feed the fountain
in the courtyard
of the playland
in those lower worlds
we are dismembered
and stacked around
decorating Kali's hall

how this world collapses
there is no perfect gauge
no ruler not distorted
no measurement unwarped
we can't converse
can't answer
because we know not what
but knowing knowing not

EMPTY WAYS DIRECTING

splintered down
wracked with visions
that are not ours
yet impinge
most direly
dragged with weights
which can not lift
beyond these depths

the hours crawl
the days fly
the concepts rot
unused, unraised
in dark dank places
which can't be plumbed
by these systems
in these times

what we hear
echoes distance
what we see
seeds old sparks
within the mind
flashing frames
from ancient sets
long lost, forgotten

the drive decays
the dream fractures
vectors fade
even as we seek to plot
their courses
roads drift with sand
and can not lead
to promised lands

our reach truncates
the open hand is severed
the striding foot mined
we seek a shelter
within our hatred
we seek a lee
in this resentment
at crushing worlds

ON TO NEW STATES

a strangeness happens
a newness comes
we can not connect
despite the depth
we can not obtain
despite the state
running in these circles
and the cycles of surprise

unfamiliar substances
now conquer time
recall collapses
everything is once
not past
not future
just at cross-hairs
the moving mark

we fall and falter
try and stumble
reach and fall away
no pattern gels
no meaning forms
only flailing
everyway within the mire
unable to sustain

locked now
frozen
systems change
the sheet of ice
shoots off from drops
slipped to the ocean
all unawares
never more the same

in completion
will we find rest?
in these cycles
will closure write?
in the yoking
to these years
will meaning flower
at last to see?

CRUSHED WITHIN THE STRIVING

spirals down
sucking vortex
gravity pits
vectors lead
into depths
into descent
to those realms
of blank despair

we thought
it might be different
we thought
there might be change
we hoped
but should have known
we prayed
but are yet damned

these days crawl
these days fly
their complexities
become defining
their challenges
put new twists
in already contorted frames
crushing us within

I can not reach
that surface world
I can not touch
the shining zone
where sleep lends substance
and blindness fills the lines
smoothing over seams
which bleed the naked light

there is no turning
of these paths
there is no shifting
of these trends
we wait the crashing
bide catastrophes
still expecting madness
to take this all away

GONE IN THIS

swept away
swept beneath
enfolded
enclosed
smothered
hidden
twisted
ruined

the systems
turn before
completion strikes
we are sampled
warped within
echoed out
scrambled
made to prophesy

these plans
form structure
these lines
drag hard
converging
seeking horizons
never found
nor at rest

such memory
pictures spin
piles overlain
on other images
other clips
tiny samples
of what once was
and never is again

broken down
discarded, scattered
we are the broken toys
on dump heaps
the dolls that have lost names
the joys that have bled out
into bitter days
cruel and no more real

ABOUT THIS COLLECTION

So many things in flux, so much change, and yet within this change so much remains the same. The strong lines persevere, often invisible, and drag things along inexplicably at the surface. We can offer no reasons, just observation and notation.

Again, this format repeats from previous collections. Of the 500 pieces written in 1994 and 1995, this represents what I consider the "best" 10%, once more presented in chronological order. Some themes and images recur poem to poem, showing themselves to be insistent memes whose demands overcome nagging aesthetic concerns for lyrical flow. Like the darkness within, they exist and must be ceded their due.

The outer world, the inner world, which is more real? The former taints the latter, seeping poisons into zones which should be pure; the latter defines the former, casting shadows where few are seen. Not even time is blameless, as it forms eddies and recycles scenes without clear point. All in all there is a sense of sinking, of a world gone bad, moving into "Some Semblance Of Decay".

- B.M.T.

www.ingramcontent.com/pod-product-compliance
Lightning Source LLC
Chambersburg PA
CBHW071741020426
42331CB00008B/2125